To Clair

God Bless you

The Power of
Renewing Your Mind

May this encourage
you to become the
greatest Version of
yourself

Venesia Williams

The author takes no responsibility for consequences as a result of actions by anyone reading this book. Before beginning this fast or any other fast, PLEASE CONSULT YOUR DOCTOR. I advise that this is not intended to provide medical advice or instruction, but for biblical principles as it relates to fasting for breakthrough.

1

The Power of Renewing Your Mind is designed to change your thought process. It is not designed to alleviate any current or future challenges, but it will help you to change your perspective and attitude in the midst of them. Throughout this devotional you will find some of the proven strategies I've personally used for myself, and my clients through my Mindset Mastery and Spiritual Mind Resuscitation coaching programs. Even now I still make it a habit to confess and speak affirmations during my daily devotion times with God. I believe this book will truly be a blessing to so many people as I was so burdened to write it as a tool to provide key strategies that will help to support anyone who wants to truly build a stronger relationship with God and be empowered to walk in their kingdom authority by overcoming fear and knowing their worth.

Maybe you're reading this book and you have been feeling stuck or struggling with anger, worry, confusion, doubt or feelings of self-condemnation. These are all attacks of the devil on your mind. One of my favorite authors, Joyce Meyers, calls it "the battlefield of the mind". Her books and teachings really encouraged me in my walk with Christ to

1

reprogram my mind and to lean not on my own understanding, but to acknowledge God in all my ways and armor myself with the Word of God daily. This empowered me to know and believe that I was no longer bound but free because whom the Son sets free, is free indeed. I always recommend her resources and encourage anyone that is struggling with their emotions or negative thoughts to read her books. I will be sharing more resources in this book that helped me on my journey. Listen, if you want what someone else has, you have to be willing to do what they did, but this will only work for you if you put in the effort.

Ask yourself the following questions and be true to yourself.

What do I spend the majority of my time thinking about?

_____

_____

_____

_____

_____

_____

Who am I?

_____

_____

_____

_____

_____

_____

What is my purpose?

_____

_____

_____

_____

_____

_____

What am I grateful for?

_____

_____

_____

_____

_____

_____

What do I love about myself?

_____

_____

_____

_____

_____

_____

It's very hard to answer these questions confidently when you don't see yourself as God sees you. **The Power of Renewing Your Mind** will teach you to find your confidence in God. I have learned in life that our self-confidence can sometimes be shaken because of how we see ourselves, but when you understand that God created you with worth and purpose, you will respect and love yourself because you respect and love God and realize you are the marvelous work of God's hands who wonderfully and fearfully made you. God accepts you when others reject you and He promises never to forsake you. He is your friend and He died for you. He loves you unconditionally.

When you acknowledge these things, you open your heart to receive His love. Knowing your worth is the foundation of self-worth. When you accept yourself, you free yourself.

There's a powerful quote by Tina Lifford that says, "When you know yourself you become empowered, but when you accept yourself, you become invincible." For me, the quality of my life is determined by the quality of my focus, so I intentionally guard my mind by focusing on the Word of God and things that are positive and good.

The Bible tells us in Philippians 4:7-9, "And the peace of God, which surpasses all understanding, will guard your hearts and your minds in Christ Jesus. Finally, brothers, whatever is true, whatever is honorable, whatever is right, whatever is pure, whatever is lovely, whatever is admirable— if anything is excellent or praiseworthy— think on these things. Whatever you have learned or received or heard from me, or seen in me, put into practice. And the God of peace will be with you."

This is a daily process you have to be consistent in doing because the devil does not want you to believe the truth and have peace of mind. He wants you to doubt and live in fear, that's why he keeps injecting lies in your mind.

2 Timothy 1:7, "For God hath not given us the spirit of fear; but of power, and of love, and of a SOUND MIND."

What does it mean to have a sound mind? Well I liked how a article I read online on FORERUNNER COMMENTARY simplified the concept of a "sound mind" stating that it has more to do with our attitude than we may realize.

According to the article,

"If our mind is sound, it is not cluttered with the cares of this world. Its processes start with God and end with God. It recognizes the power of God and His love for us. However, having and maintaining a sound mind requires constant work, a positive approach, and an acceptance of both the good and the bad. It needs continual stirring like a simmering pot on the stove. We have to guard it and exercise it at all times. A sound mind recognizes that we are special to God, not from our own strength but because of the gift of His Holy Spirit. Even though we may be only one person and insignificant, we must have the kind of mind that takes charge of itself and moves forward, not in retreat as many of God's people are doing today. God is a very positive God who looks forward to the future and the promises of having us as a key part of His creation. This begins by developing a personal relationship with Him daily. A major part of this journey is renewing your mind. You will have to learn about His ways as you grow and mature in Him you will become more and more like Him."

Jeremiah 29:11, *"For I know the plans I have for you,"* declares the Lord, *"plans to prosper you and not harm you, plans to give you hope and a future."*

You can do all things through Christ who strengthens you. Do you know that you have restitution in Christ? What was once lost in the Garden of Eden has now been restored to you through Christ. He is doing a new thing through His finished works. He has given you keys to the kingdom to bind and loose.

According to His Word in Matthew 16:19, *"I will give you the keys of the kingdom of heaven; whatever you bind on earth will be bound in heaven, and whatever you loose on earth will be loosed in heaven."*

You have dominion over the earth and access to fellowship with God. According to Genesis 1:26, "In the beginning God created Adam in his own image and likeness." God's original plan has always been for us to fellowship with Him by knowing who we are in Him and to break free from having a slavery mindset and begin thinking like a son of God. This can only happen when we walk in biblical truth and stop coming in agreement with the lies of the enemy. 1 Peter 2:9 reminds us about who we are according to His Word, not our situation or how we may be feeling. It reads, *"You are a chosen generation, a royal priesthood, a holy nation, a peculiar people; that you should show forth praise of him who hath called you out of darkness into his marvelous light."*

Roman 8:16-17, *"The Spirit Himself testifies with our spirit that we are God's children. And if we are children, then we are heirs: heirs of God and co-heirs with Christ— if indeed we suffer with Him, so that we may also be glorified with Him."*

As sons of God we have been called out of darkness and into marvelous light. Darkness cannot have you any more. I know you must be thinking that's easier said than done, and yes, you are completely right, but if you continue to speak it, you will see the light and you will no longer want to remain in darkness. In my book Turning Point I share a number of things that occurred throughout my life that had me mentally imprisoned in a dark place. Yes, it is possible to be free physically and chained mentally if you don't allow light into your mind. The Word of God is a lamp to our feet and a light to our path, so we need the Word to stop us from stumbling in darkness, to guide us and to open the eyes of our understanding. There are some things that are only revealed when you move out of the situation.

Ephesians 4:17-24 (NKJV),

> "This I say, therefore, and testify in the Lord,
> that you should no longer walk as [a] the rest
> of the Gentiles walk, in the futility of their
> mind, having their understanding darkened,
> being alienated from the life of God, because
> of the ignorance that is in them, because of
> the blindness of their heart; who, being past
> feeling, have given themselves over to
> lewdness, to work all uncleanness with
> greediness. But you have not so learned
> Christ, if indeed you have heard Him and have
> been taught by Him, as the truth is in Jesus:
> that you put off, concerning your former
> conduct, the old man which grows corrupt
> according to the deceitful lusts and be
> renewed in the spirit of your mind, and that
> you put on the new man which was created
> according to God, in true righteousness and
> holiness."

The old man has to die, so the new man can live, meaning all things become new. To transform means to change completely in composition or structure. For example, a caterpillar transforms into a butterfly. When you renew your mind, you transform your entire life, and you become a complete person, and who God has designed you to be.

2 Corinthian 5:17, *"If anyone is in Christ, he is a new creation, old things have passed away; behold, all things have become new."*

Insanity is doing the same thing over and over again, and expecting a new result. I hear the Lord saying, "It is time to shift out of that old mindset and shift out of that old place because it is no longer conducive for your growth." Your old place has reached its maximum capacity. God is preparing you for more. Just as an old wine skin has been used and stretched so much that it is no longer flexible or usable, if you refuse to shift into your new season you will remain limited, stagnant and unable to maximize your full potential and fulfill your God given purpose.

Just like you cannot pour new wine into old wine skin, you cannot bring your old season into your new season. It is time to shift out of the old and embrace the new. You are being shifted into another place and another level. When God begins to blow on your life, a fresh wind is released to shift your life, your spirit and your heart.

Declare it out loud now- I am shifting into my new!

New Mindset, New Excitement, New Experiences, New Fire, New Appetite, New Revelation, New Anointing, New Mercy, New Grace, New Strength,

New Praise, New Worship, New Wine, New Oil, New Connection, New Money, New Blessings, New Favour, New Season, and New Me!

I pray throughout this 21-day journey of transformation, that the power of the living Word of God will cleanse you, remold you, renew you, restore you and set you free by changing you from the inside out. When God lives within you, you are spiritually reborn, and have become a new creation. I thank God that you don't have to do it by yourself or rely on your own strength or power because He has sent you The Holy Spirit who is the Helper. He helps you to understand and apply God's Word to your life. He guides you into all truth and helps you to obey God. Be confident in God by knowing that you have everything you need in Him for this journey.

It takes 21 days to break a habit, which is why I know it is only by the Spirit of God that I received theses key strategies for you today. I remember growing up as a young child my mother would always tell me that habits are easy to make, but hard to break, so try to make habits that you won't need to break.

I want to encourage you today that you have the power within you to replace every unhealthy cycle in your life with new, healthy cycles. I hear the Lord saying He is breaking unhealthy cycles. Break free from toxic relationships, addictions, sexual immorality, mistaken identity, sickness, procrastination and confusion in your life. As you go on this 21-day journey of renewing your mind and transforming your life, I pray that you will be empowered with a winning mindset and experience victory in every area of your life. Your mind is constantly gaining new information. It never stops thinking. Even when you are not thinking, you are still thinking without thinking. Your mind is always gathering new ideas and thoughts, as well as thoughts from your past, present and future. Your mind will remind you of your past hurt, pain and trauma from something that happened in your childhood and it will feel like it happened yesterday. This is why it is so important to guard and direct your mind and to be willing to arrest every negative thought that comes to steal your joy and peace. The Word of God encourages us to purify our minds by washing it with the Word, arresting every evil imagination and pulling down every stronghold that rises up.

Ephesians 5:26 (KJV), *"That he might sanctify and cleanse it with the washing of water by the word."*

2 Corinthians 10:5 (KJV) *"Casting down imaginations, and every high thing that exalteth itself against the knowledge of God, and bringing into captivity every thought to the obedience of Christ."*

The worst thing you can do is become comfortable with negative or self-defeating thoughts. The Bible says that we must think on things that are lovely and pure and of good report because whatever you feed your mind, is what it will produce in your life. The battle is won or lost in your mind. As you learn who you are in Christ, you will find throughout this process that your mind will be renewed and your old ways of thinking will be replaced by the truth of God's Word if you commit to following and applying the strategies given to you in this book.

You can change your tomorrow by starting today. I just want to let you know that you are not alone. I have personally been there myself and coached hundreds of people that were right where you are now. Are you wondering why me? Why does it feel like I am continuously fighting a losing battle against feelings of fear, doubt, unworthiness, anxiety or depression? It is time to dismantle the schemes of the enemy and recognize the lies of the enemy floating around in your mind, and replace them with the truth of God.

Discover over the next 21 days how to defend your mind against the attacks of the enemy and receive the mind of Christ. Satan is already defeated. It was all done for you on the cross through the blood of Jesus Christ. He paid the price for you in full. This book will empower you to receive God's transformational power in your life. Implementing the strategies in my own life has helped me to evolve as a daughter, mother, sibling, friend, senior leader, speaker, entrepreneur, mentor/coach and future best-selling author. Changing the way I think has honesty pushed me to grow a closer and deeper relationship with God and liberated me in my mind, will and emotions.

Transformation does not come from putting on a suit or a long skirt. So many times people only focus on changing their outward garments and never changing their hearts or renewing their minds. God desires us to be transformed, not conformed. Transformation happens internally by taking the time out to be honest with one's self. I encourage all of my clients to journal and keep a diary of their spiritual growth and personal development. It is important that you examine yourself and evaluate your progress by setting achievable long-term and short-term goals, and set daily, weekly and monthly targets that will help you to accomplish them. You have to start preparing for where you are going, not where you have been or where you currently are. Changing your perspective will determine if you fly like a butterfly or remain crawling in a low place like a caterpillar.

Do you see yourself with wings?

_____

_____

_____

Are you surrounded by caterpillars or butterflies?

_____

_____

_____

If you are only around caterpillars, you will stay low to fit in because it's familiar and easier, but if you are around butterflies you will desire to grow your wings and develop, stretch and maximize your full potential.

Roman 8:16-17, _"The Spirit Himself testifies with our spirit that we are God's children. And if we are children, then we are heirs: heirs of God and co-heirs with Christ— if indeed we suffer with Him, so that we may also be glorified with Him."_

What are you feeding your mind?

_____

_____

_____

What are you reading?

_____

_____

_____

What are you watching?

_____

_____

How do you spend your time?

_____

_____

_____

Who do you spend your time with?

_____

_____

_____

Ephesians 4:23-24 (NLT), _"Let the Spirit renew your thoughts and attitudes, put on your new nature created to be like God- truly righteous and holy."_

God wants to transform you into His original design. You are a masterpiece of His love, mercy and grace and an exhibition of His transformational power. God is a master at turning things around, which I go into great detail about in my first book TURNING POINT – How God Turned My Darkness into Marvelous Light, as I describe how he turned things around in my life. He is a master at turning your mess into a masterpiece.

The Power of Renewing Your Mind is strategically designed to give you practical steps to put into action and free you from the bondage of mental strongholds once and for all by renewing your mind through the Word of God and aligning with the

Word of God. The only thing standing in the way of God's plans for your life is you! In order to rebuild your life, you have to be willing to be intentional about rebuilding your mindset, because your thoughts control your emotions, and your emotions control your actions, and your actions control your destiny. You cannot allow your emotions and thoughts to steal your victory. So many Christians need to be converted to **BELIEVERS** because one of the biggest obstacles standing in the way of seeing God's transformational power in their lives is their mindset and lack of belief.

How many times have you been guilty of hearing the Word of God and allowing your thoughts and emotions to kill the very Word you just received?

God is not just concerned with your actions; He is concerned with your thoughts too. The truth of the matter is that your thoughts will betray you and rob you of your joy and peace if you are not willing to put in the work and renew your mind daily. The Word of God encourages us not to be conformed to the world, but to be transformed by the renewing of our minds, daily focusing on what is the good and acceptable, perfect will of God.

Romans 12:2 (AMP), *"And do not be conformed to this world [any longer with its superficial values and* customs], but be [a] transformed and progressively changed [as you mature spiritually] by the renewing of your mind [focusing on godly values and ethical attitudes], so that you may prove [for yourselves] what the will of God is, that which is good and acceptable and perfect [in His plan and purpose for you]."

Many of our thoughts are inspired by past experiences, pain, brokenness and emotions that we have not surrendered to God. We cannot heal from what we conceal or fail to confront. If you want to conquer something, you have to confront it head on. Throughout my time coaching and mentoring people, I have come across many people who fall into the trap of thinking they have no control over how they feel or think when a wave of emotions floods their mind with negative, self-defeating thoughts or they are faced with a challenging situation and start to feel powerless to change any of it. God has not left you powerless. He has given you the Holy Spirit.

Psalms 51:10, "Create in me a clean heart, O God, and renew a steadfast Spirit within me."

Ephesians 4 clearly tells us to, "Let the SPIRIT RENEW OUR THOUGHTS." This means we have to learn how to depend on the SPIRIT of God, not our own strength, power or might, but His HOLY SPIRIT who has been sent to teach us all things. The Holy Spirit brings the Word of God to life and makes it our reality, so if it doesn't align with the Word of God, then it is not our reality. With the help of the Holy Spirit, you can finally learn how to control your negative thoughts and emotions and stop letting them control you. Jesus has left you the Comforter, who is the Holy Spirit, to help you. Choose today not to worry about anything, but to trust God with everything by surrendering all to the Spirit of truth to guide you and teach you.

According to John 16:13, "*But when he, the Spirit of truth, comes, he will guide you into all the truth. He will not speak on his own; he will speak only what he hears, and he will tell you what is yet to come.*"

There is a constant war between good and evil in our minds. God wants to lift us up, and the enemy wants to press us down.

According to Paul in Romans 7: 18-20, "*I know that nothing good lives in me, that is, in my flesh; for I have the desire to do what is good, but I cannot carry it out. For I do not do the good I want to do. Instead, I keep on doing the evil I do not want to do. And if I do what I do not want, it is no longer I who do it, but it is sin living in me that does it.*"

19

This scripture shows us how important it is to be disciplined, to take authority over our lives and to resist the devil so that he can flee, by being led by the Spirit and not the flesh, and letting the anointing break every yoke and release us from bondage.

You may be thinking to yourself what is bondage? Bondage is basically anything that has power over you. For example, unhealthy cycles, addictions, sexual immorality, greed, and lust, are all a form of bondage. As a result of sin, the desires of the flesh can leave us struggling with depression, fear, doubt, insecurities, and unbelief, and trapped in a self-inflicted prison in our minds, causing us to crave for the very things that are killing us spiritually- mind, body and soul, because you can never satisfy your flesh. In order to live a life of abundance, we must live a life of prayer and fasting.

As Mark 9:29 says, *"And he said to them, This kind can come forth by nothing, but by PRAYER and FASTING."*

Fasting allows you to deny your fleshly desires and cravings to focus on feeding your spirit instead of your body, bringing you closer to God. The enemy comes to kill, steal and destroy, but God, as recorded in John 10:10 came that we might have life, and life more abundantly. As you are on this journey of transformation, I encourage you to fast and pray as you follow the strategies given to you in this 21-day devotional.

2

It's time to break out of limitations and break free from every spirit of limitation in our lives in Jesus Name. God is releasing a breakers anointing through these pages to empower you to walk in the power and authority given to you through Christ. Proverbs 18: 21 clearly says that we have the POWER of LIFE and DEATH in our tongues and we will eat the fruits of our lips, so don't allow your mouth to block your blessings or stop your breakthrough.

Proverb 18:21, *"Life and death are in the power of the tongue, and those who love it will eat its fruit."*

What are you saying to yourself?

What are you saying about your situation?

What are you saying about your ability?

What are you saying about your purpose?

You have power and authority to bind and to loose. You are free in Jesus Christ and have been redeemed in Him to have LIBERTY.

22

Psalm 46:1, *"God is our refuge and strength and ever-present help in trouble."*

Don't give into the worries of life entering your mind today. Whether it be a loved one battling sickness, addictions, an unruly child or unpaid bills, remember that God is your refuge and your strength. He hears your cry, and He is a good shepherd. Cast your burdens on Him today. Let go of your past or current situations. Trust God to be your Helper in times of trouble. Learn to rely on Him and give Him your whole heart. Allow Him to filter your heart daily through prayer and meditating on His Word.

The Bible says that as a man thinketh in his heart, so is he. So how we think in our hearts will manifest in our lives. You have to stop saying the wrong things, and start saying the right things. If we focus on our limitations, we will live a very limited life, and if we focus on progression, we will live a very progressive life.

You have to discipline yourself to pray. Praying consistently builds up your spiritual muscles and keeps you in alignment with the will, plans and purposes of God. Prayer is communication between you and God. It's a divine conversation with our heavenly father. Prayer works by talking to God and Him talking back to you. It is about relationship, not religion. Remaining consistent in prayer is the key to retraining your mind and living life in abundance.

Our lives are controlled by what we focus on and what we say. You have the power to speak what you want to see manifest in your life. The Bible tells us to focus on the things that are of good report and to be anxious over nothing. We have become a new creation in Christ. It is important that we take off the old man, and put on the new man. By renewing our minds, we will be transformed in Christ through the Word of God. We have to make a choice to let the Spirit of God control us, so that we can be fruitful believers and bear good fruits. We cannot do it on our own- we need to abide in Him. According to John 15, we must be intentional about spending quality time with God, meditating on His word and living a lifestyle of prayer and fasting.

John 15:4-6 (NKJV), *"Abide in Me, and I in you. As the branch cannot bear fruit of itself, unless it abides in the vine, neither can you, unless you abide in Me. I am the vine; you are the branches. He who abides in Me, and I in him, bears much fruit; for without Me you can do nothing. If anyone does not abide in Me, he is cast out as a branch and is withered; and they gather them and throw them into the fire, and they are burned."*

There is so much power in renewing your mind and knowing the Word of God! Freedom begins in the mind.

24

According to Luke 15:11-32,

Jesus continued: "There was a man who had two sons. The younger one said to his father, 'Father, give me my share of the estate.' So he divided his property between them." Not long after that, the younger son got together all he had, set off for a distant country and there squandered his wealth in wild living. After he had spent everything, there was a severe famine in that whole country, and he began to be in need. So he went and hired himself out to a citizen of that country, who sent him to his fields to feed pigs. He longed to fill his stomach with the pods that the pigs were eating, but no one gave him anything. "When he came to his senses, he said, 'How many of my father's hired servants have food to spare, and here I am starving to death! I will set out and go back to my father and say to him: Father, I have sinned against heaven and against you. I am no longer worthy to be called your son; make me like one of your hired servants.' So he got up and went to his father. "But while he was still a long way off, his father saw him and was filled with compassion for him; he ran to his son, threw his arms around him and kissed him. "The son said to

25

him, 'Father, I have sinned against heaven and against you. I am no longer worthy to be called your son.' "But the father said to his servants, 'Quick! Bring the best robe and put it on him. Put a ring on his finger and sandals on his feet. Bring the fattened calf and kill it. Let's have a feast and celebrate. For this son of mine was dead and is alive again; he was lost and is found.' So they began to celebrate. "Meanwhile, the older son was in the field. When he came near the house, he heard music and dancing. So he called one of the servants and asked him what was going on. 'Your brother has come,' he replied, 'and your father has killed the fattened calf because he has him back safe and sound.' "The older brother became angry and refused to go in. So his father went out and pleaded with him. But he answered his father, 'Look! All these years I've been slaving for you and never disobeyed your orders. Yet you never gave me even a young goat so I could celebrate with my friends. But when this son of yours who has squandered your property with prostitutes comes home, you kill the fattened calf for him!'

"'My son,' the father said, 'you are always with me, and everything I have is yours. But we had to celebrate and be glad, because this brother of yours was dead and is alive again; he was lost and is found.

Freedom begins in your mindset, but you have to embrace the internal freedom you have externally. It is possible to be free physically, and chained mentally. Many of us can relate to the prodigal son. How many times have we tried to plan our own course in life and disregarded God's leading? Things started to run good for a while, but then things started to derail and become dysfunctional. Things started to feel like it was all failing apart and you reach that moment of clarity, almost like turning on a bright light. Now you can see how foolish you have been, and you recognize that doing things your way has caused you to drift away from God and into sin.

This is the turning point, when you can turn back to God and turn away from sin. That's what the prodigal son did. He returned back to His father. He returned back to love, and he returned back to life. He came back to his senses. All that's standing in your way of turning now is pride. We need to acknowledge that God knows best. You cannot live a satisfied life without God. Sometimes we can allow things or people to pull us away from God, so we have to take responsibility for the role we played in things that failed- this could be relationships, careers, and businesses that didn't honor him.

God is the father in this parable. He's there

with open arms ready to offer His love and mercy for your failures. He's ready to restore you as his child and cover you with his blessings. The father never stops giving and forgiving those who depend on Him.

1 Corinthians 13:5, *"It does not dishonor others, it is not self-seeking, it is not easily angered, it keeps no record of wrongs."*

One of the hardest things you will ever have to do is cast down your idols, the things you have knowingly or unknowingly put before God. The enemy is attacking your thoughts and belief systems because he doesn't want you to know your value and your worth. Everything starts in the mind, this is why I have such a passion to empower people to believe in themselves, to think bigger and to remove all barriers and limitations from their lives, teaching them to find confidence in God's living and everlasting Word and eternal life found in Christ.

Don't settle for less when you know you deserve more, you are worth it!

Understanding yourself better will help you to ACCEPT those things you like least about yourself.

Liking yourself will help you to RESPECT yourself.

Being confident in yourself will help you to find new ways to ENJOY yourself.
Loving yourself will help you to love others as you love yourself.

3

God is love, and love is God.

The Bible commands us to LOVE. It is the greatest gift of all. According to 1 Corinthians 13:13, "So these three things will forever endure; remain: FAITH, HOPE AND LOVE and the greatest of all three is love."

Mark 12:30-31 *"Love the LORD your God with all your heart and with all your soul and with all your mind and with all your strength.' The second is this: 'Love your neighbor as yourself.' There is no commandment greater than these."*

Love yourself enough to free yourself and protect your peace! Some people are not bad people they are just not good for you in the season you are in. Some people actually come into your life, not to stay, but to introduce you to someone else who will stay.
I want to encourage you to appreciate the baby steps. Appreciation is the key to growth. Before I give you the five key steps to renewing your mind, I would like you to answer the questions below to help you

refocus your mind and evaluate how you see yourself.

How would you describe yourself?

_____

_____

_____

What do you like best about yourself?

_____

_____

_____

What are your strengths?

_____

_____

_____

What are your skills and talents?

_____

_____

_____

How open are you to new experiences?

_____

_____

_____

What do you least like about yourself?

_____

_____

_____

Name 3 ways you can work on improving the thing or things you least like about yourself.

_____

_____

_____

How committed are you to what you say?

_____

_____

_____

Why are you committed?

_____

_____

_____

Now when things get difficult or you are facing the storms of life, please remember your why. Your why is everything!

Many people are facing storms right now that have been set by the devil to destroy them.

John 10:10 (NIV), *"The thief comes to only steal and kill and destroy; I have come that they may have life, and have it to the full."*

The devil will start by attacking the mind, which will lead to harmful effects in your body and soul. Your soul is your mind, will and emotions. This is his ultimate goal, to have you feeling overwhelmed with stress, and causing tension that could then open up the door to other health issues like headaches, high blood pressure, anxiety, acid reflux, panic attacks, ulcers, and gastrointestinal problems. The stress will take ahold of your body, and cause a domino effect.

This is why it is so important that you understand why renewing your mind is critical to the well being of your mind, body and soul. If your mind is filled with self-defeating, negative thoughts about yourself and others, you are playing right into the devil's hands. He wants you to be unbalanced mentally, falling apart physically and growing more and more weary day by day. I know you're thinking, "Venesia, I don't want to think like this. I've tried so many times and it's hard to remove these thoughts out of my mind on my own."

Stop right there. You are not alone; God is with you. In Psalm 27 He says, *"Even if your mother and father forsake you, He would never forsake you."*

This is just what the devil wants you to think, so that you will start questioning God and doubting His transformational power to set you free.

1 Peter 5:8 (NIV) tells us to, *"Be alert and of sober mind. Your enemy the devil prowls around like a roaring lion looking for someone to devour."*

The power of renewing your mind gives you the solution you need to heal your mind, body and soul from the attacks of the enemy, which is why reading God's word daily to cleanse you, empower you and transform you is essential. I encourage you to use the promises of God as daily affirmations and prayer points. As you continue reading, I will share some that you can implement in your life.

You have to take the time to feed yourself spiritually as much as you feed yourself physically. I once heard someone say that what you feed will grow and what you starve will die, so by feeding your spirit you are killing your flesh.

Who is controlling your thoughts?

Is the enemy controlling your thoughts?

Or is the Holy Spirit controlling your thoughts?

When you put your faith in Christ and His word, you will hear the inaudible, see the invisible and achieve the impossible. Everything that appears in the natural world must first exist in the spirit.

Hebrews 11:1 (NKJV), *"Now faith is the substances of things hoped for, the evidence of things not seen."* *Putting your faith in Christ will help you to overcome your past, empower your present and unfold your future.*

Ephesians 3:19, *"And to know the love of Christ that surpasses knowledge, that you may be filled with all the fullness of God."*

Are you open to receiving the love of God? There is length, width, height and depth to his love. God loves you and created you in his image. I used to think that once I reached a certain level of maturity in Christ I would never have to experience any more negative thoughts or feelings of fear, doubt, anger or resentment. Being saved and having these thoughts can cause you to feel even more guilty, and lead to you beating yourself up because of your thought life. The truth is WE need the HOLY SPIRIT to control our thoughts. You do not have to accept every single thought that comes into your mind. Just because you have a negative thought, doesn't mean you have to accept it, receive it or believe it. You can reject it, renounce it and replace it with a positive thought or the Word of God. We have to intentionally reclaim our minds, and begin to see it as a territory with a constant battle between the Holy Spirit and the enemy. You have to decide who you will give territory to.

James 4:7-8, *"Submit yourselves, then to God. Resist the devil and he will flee from you. Draw near to God and He will draw near to you, cleanse your hands, you sinners and purify your hearts you doubleminded."*

Given your mind is where your spiritual transformation happens, are you surprised that the enemy is fighting continuously to take territory? You have to begin reclaiming the territory of your mind for the Lord by recognizing the little attacks. Don't you realize that many of the negative thoughts you are thinking aren't actually yours? Many of your negative thoughts are lies that the devil is trying to get you to accept as truth.

Why does he plant these seeds in our thoughts?
He wants to stir up your emotions. He knows that if he can manipulate your emotions, he can get you to miss out on something that God has in store for you.

The devil has been studying you for a long time, enough to know what things you will believe. He knows your past pain and your past failures. He even knows your past hurt and who caused you to feel rejected, abandoned or insecure.

What are you meditating on?

_____

_____

_____

What kinds of thoughts are consuming your mind?

_____

_____

_____

Is the enemy taking over territory or the Holy Spirit?

_____

_____

_____

Negative self-defeating thoughts caused by the enemy usually start with:
- I can't
- I'm not good enough
- I'm not qualified
- I'm going to fail

Who's Voice Are You Listening to?

Because the enemy knows you, he knows the kind of seed to plant that you will consider and that closely resembles the truth. He also knows the kind of things that you won't believe. He often whispers things linked to your past pain, hurt or trauma. Lies only produce more lies. He whispers them to you repeatedly because he wants you to believe that they are your own thoughts, and he wants you to accept his lies and truth. The enemy sows bad seeds and while men sleep he sows tares by releasing multiple voices like the:

- Voice of doubt
- Voice of fear
- Voice of anxiety
- Voice of insecurity
- Voice of torment
- Voice of hopelessness

Matthew 13:24-25, *"Jesus put before them another parable: "The kingdom of heaven is like a man who sowed good seed in his field. But while everyone was asleep, his enemy came and sowed weeds among the wheat, and slipped away."*

You cannot allow the devil's lies to become more real to you than God's truth. Learn to examine the source of your thoughts. In Genesis 3 we see a clear example of how the enemy mixes his lies with the truth to plant seeds of doubt and to draw us into disobedience, which ultimately delays or distracts us.

"Now the serpent was more crafty than any beast of the field which the LORD God had made. And he said to the woman, "Indeed, has God said, 'You shall not eat from any tree of the garden'?" And the woman said to the serpent, "From the fruit of the trees of the garden we may eat; but from the fruit of the tree which is in the middle of the garden, God has said, 'You shall not eat from it or touch it, lest you die.'" And the serpent said to the woman, "You surely shall not die! For God knows that in the day you eat from it your eyes will be opened, and you will be like God, knowing good and evil." When the woman saw that the tree was good for food, and that it was a delight to the eyes, and that the tree was desirable to make one wise, she took from its fruit and ate; and she gave also to her husband with her, and he ate." -Genesis 3:1-6

Genesis 3 states one thing about the serpent, that he was very crafty. All the other things that are stated about him are revealed later on, but at this point they are kept hidden from the reader. Instead, we are introduced to the serpent through what he does. "You shall know them by their fruit (Matthew 7:16, 20)."The Lord wants us to understand that it is more important to discern false words than to know the source of them. Unfortunately, we spend more time learning about false sources and thought.

The serpent speaking to Eve in the Garden was not innocent or good in any sense of the meaning. He accomplished his purpose largely through deceit. He tricked her into believing his lies, instead of God's truth. He placed a thought in her mind, which she began to lust after and desire, which caused her to disobey God. This is why we need to be trained in the truth of God's Word and the power of renewing our mind.

Genesis 3:1, ""Has God indeed (really) said, "You shall not eat of every tree of the garden?""

The serpent, using crafty questioning, covered up his motive and led Eve to doubt her trust in God. We cannot say that he lied because it was a question, but in fact he planted some false thoughts, which he used to confuse her. The fact was that God had given all the trees except one to eat from, but his question caused her to think that God had withheld the best from her.

Genesis 3:4-5, "You will not surely die. For God knows that in the day that you eat of it your eyes will be opened, and you will be like God, knowing good and evil."

The serpent goes much further here than in the first twisting of God's word. In this second scripture he went to outright denial and contradiction of what God had earlier expressed to them. As yet they did not know death, and they had not lost the fellowship of God. They trusted that God loved them and meant what He said. They believed that God had their welfare in mind, until the serpent spoke in outright contradiction to God's word. Eve knew and practiced God's Word, but an enticing promise caught her attention. Note the nature of the promise. You do not have a way of testing it without disobeying or disregarding God's clear warning against it.

This is important with regard to tempting thoughts. Satan tries to plant deceiving thoughts in your mind to give you the impression that they are your own thoughts, and if you keep them there long enough they will eventually become your own thoughts and the enemy will gain territory. This is why it's important to immediately pull down and cast out any negative, self-defeating, tempting or ungodly thoughts. Do not meditate on them or allow the lying seeds of the enemy to grow into trees. It's much easier to uproot a seed planted, than it is to cut down and dig up a tree that's been rooted and grounded within you. You uproot the seed planted by, as I will repeatedly keep saying, replacing the lies of the enemy with the truth in the word of God.

The serpent is very creepy and patient. As we can see in the Word of God, he creeps in gradually. In one short moment, this stranger causes all this doubt to fly through her formerly pure mind. Perhaps we underestimate the impact thoughts can have on our minds even when we do not "believe" them. We need to recognize the source of our thoughts, uproot the seeds planted by the enemy and replace it with the Word of God. This 21-day devotional will teach you to do just this, by illustrating how to speak scriptures over your life that contradicts the lies of the enemy.

John 10:4-5(NKJV), *"And when he brings out his own sheep, he goes before them; and the sheep follow him, for they know his voice. Yet they will by no means follow a stranger, but will flee from him, for they do not know the voice of strangers."*

Jesus wisely reminds us to seek extra protection from these temptations in the Lord's Prayer, "And do not lead us into temptation, but deliver us from evil Matthew 6:13)." Let's look closer at the reason why Eve submitted to the evil one. Genesis 3:6 reveals three clear reasons as to why Eve was persuaded-good for food; pleasant to the eye; and desirable to make one wise.

As you look at some of your past or current temptations, you may attempt to identify how the enemy was able to creep in and influence you. You may even be wondering to yourself, "If God loves me so much, why did He let this happen to me?"

Genesis 3:1-6 records God's test for man. God did not tempt man. The Lord wants man to succeed using all his resources, experiences and devotion to follow in obedience and be richly rewarded. Instead, we find that Eve is deceived and falls into sin, while Adam, not being deceived, turns his heart away from God and onto his own desires by following his wife. Together they lead humankind into sin.

Studying this passage of scripture really gave me an understanding of our connection to God. God desires to fellowship with us daily and through Christ what was lost in the Garden of Eden has been restored to us. We have restitution. Adam and Eve may not have died physically, but they did die spiritually, which resulted in the loss of their spiritual authority and connection with God.

Genesis 3:8-10, "8Then the man and his wife heard the sound of the LORD God as he was walking in the garden in the cool of the day, and they hid from the LORD God among the trees of the garden. 9But the LORD God called to the man, "Where are you?" 10He answered, "I heard you in the garden, and I was afraid because I was naked; so I hid."

God knew where Adam was physically, but could not locate him spiritually. God's original plan has always been to fellowship with us. From the beginning, we were designed to take dominion over the earth that He created as sons of God.

Romans 8:19-21, *"For the creation waits in eager expectation for the children of God to be revealed. For the creation was subjected to frustration, not by its own choice, but by the will of the one who subjected it, in hope that the creation itself will be liberated from its bondage to decay and brought into the freedom and glory of the children of God."*

This is done by first being born again and then by knowing who you are in Christ. This is so important to maintaining your walk with Christ and exercising your power and authority as sons of God, so that you won't be derailed by the enemy, but instead will stay in total alignment with God and His Word by having a relationship with Him.

After Adam sinned he hid from God. I want to encourage you today, if you are in a fallen place, do not remain there. Instead repent and run back to God.

Romans 6:23, *"For the wages of sin is death, but the gift of God is eternal life in Christ Jesus our Lord."*

Jesus our Lord is the lamb of God that takes away the sin of the world. Adam's disobedience caused a disconnection between his spirit and the Spirit of God. As a result, Adam and Eve began to live out of their soul (mind, will and emotions) instead of their spirit. Your mind is valuable territory. If the enemy can control your thoughts, he can control your emotions and your actions; and his lies can influence your actions if you do not take authority over them.

How Can We Stop This?

We can learn a powerful lesson by studying Jesus Christ.
According to Hebrews 4:15-16 (NLT), *"This High Priest of ours understands our weaknesses, for he faced all of the same testings we do, yet he did not sin. So let us come boldly to the throne of our gracious God. There we will receive his mercy, and we will find grace to help us when we need it most."*

Jesus is our example. We can trust Him to guide us. He chose to come here to go through the things we went through on a daily basis, and he overcame them to empower us to have victory. Sometimes it's easy to forget that Jesus faced the same challenges that we come up against every day. Satan's tricks have not changed. He only recycles them over and over again and reuses them. He's been pulling the same old tricks, schemes and plots since the fall of man.

This is the question that I always ask myself personally before making any decisions...**What Would Jesus Do?**

Jesus had to deal with Satan's tricks too when he was tempted by the devil in the wilderness after his 40 day fast.

Matthew 4:1-11,

> "Then Jesus was led up by the Spirit into the wilderness to be tempted by the devil. And when He had fasted forty days and forty nights, afterward He was hungry. Now when the tempter came to Him, he said, "If You are the Son of God, command that these stones become bread." But He answered and said, "It is written, 'Man shall not live by bread alone, but by every word that proceeds from the mouth of God. " Then the devil took Him up into the holy city, set Him on the pinnacle of the temple, and said to Him, "If You are the Son of God, throw Yourself down. For it is written:'He shall give His angels charge over you,'and,'In their hands they shall bear you up, Lest you dash your foot against a stone. " Jesus said to him, "It is written again, 'You shall not [a]tempt the Lord your God.' "Again, the devil took Him up on an exceedingly high mountain, and showed Him all the kingdoms of the world and their glory. And he said to

Him, "All these things I will give You if You will fall down and worship me." Then Jesus said to him, [b]"Away with you, Satan! For it is written, 'You shall worship the Lord your God, and Him only you shall serve." Then the devil left Him, and behold, angels came and ministered to Him."

Jesus implemented the strategy I am teaching you here.

- Jesus resisted the devil.
- Jesus rebuked the devil
- Jesus replaced the devil's lies with the TRUTH of the WORD OF GOD.

Jesus is our perfect example of how to be victorious over our thoughts and bring them into submission to our Father. Right before the crucifixion, Jesus knew His destiny. He knew his date with the cross, and He knew the suffering He would face. His suffering is central in God's plan to redeem man from sin.

All of the Old Testament sacrifices were constant reminders of sin and its result in death. Blood sacrifices were made according to Leviticus 17:11 which says, "For the life of a creature is in the blood, and I have given it to you to make atonement for yourselves on the altar; it is the blood that makes atonement for one's life."

Redemption was his suffering and death on the cross. It is His sacrificial death that makes atonement for sins and brings redemption.

1 John 5:13, *"I write these things to you who believe in the name of the Son of God so that you may know that you have eternal life."*

Your destiny does not have to be a mystery. Apostle John wrote clearly in 1 John 5:12, " Whoever has the Son has life; whoever does not have the Son of God does not have life."

Your destiny is determined by your personal relationship with God. According to Romans 8:1, there is no condemnation to those who are in Christ Jesus.

John 3:14-21,

"Just as Moses lifted up the snake in the wilderness, so the Son of Man must be lifted up, that everyone who believes may have eternal life in him." For God so loved the world that he gave his one and only Son, that whoever believes in him shall not perish but have eternal life. For God did not send his Son into the world to condemn the world, but to save the world through him. Whoever believes in him is not condemned, but whoever does not believe stands condemned already because they have not believed in the name of God's one and only Son. This is the verdict: Light has come into the world, but people loved darkness instead of light because their deeds were evil. Everyone who does evil hates the light, and will not come into the light for fear that their deeds will be exposed. But whoever lives by the truth comes into the light, so that it may be seen plainly that what they have done has been done in the sight of God."

Can you imagine the thoughts and emotions that were going through the mind of Christ? As it grew closer to the time leading up to the cross, his human emotions began to creep in, and His soul was crushed.

According to Mark 14:32-36,"*They went to a place called Gethsemane, and Jesus said to his disciples, "Sit here while I pray."He took Peter, James and John along with him, and he began to be deeply distressed and troubled. "My soul is overwhelmed with sorrow to the point of death," he said to them. "Stay here and keep watch." Going a little farther, he fell to the ground and prayed that if possible the hour might pass from him. "Abba, Father," he said, "everything is possible for you. Take this cup from me. Yet not what I will, but what you will."*

49

Jesus knew what was at stake and He knew that Satan was using his emotions against him. If he did not regain control, He would not only be sacrificing his own victory over the cross but all of ours as well. Sometimes we don't realize what is at stake or how valuable we are to God and his plans and purposes on earth. Just like Jesus it is important that we know what is at stake. Jesus knew what you must learn. His mind was a battlefield. If He gave up that valuable territory, we would all lose the war. Jesus humbled himself and was obedient unto death, and for this very reason God exalted Him and gave Him the name above every other name. Jesus having taken a form of man demonstrated to us how we should behave.

How did he fight?

What did he do?

Mark 14:35-36 teaches us how Jesus fought His mind battles. The scripture reads, "Going a little farther, he fell to the ground and prayed that if possible the hour might pass from him." Abba, Father," he said, "everything is possible for you. Take this cup from me. Yet not what I will, but what you will."

Jesus said I want your will to be done above my will. He lived in total submission to His father in heaven. This teaches us that God's will is so much greater than ours. No matter how we may be feeling, we need to decide whose will we are going to stand for? Jesus wanted the coming torment and pain to be taken away, His emotions were kicking in and He wanted out of God's plan, but more than all of that He wanted God's will to be done.

4

You cannot pour the newness of who you are becoming into the oldness of who you used to be. You have to break familiarity to embrace the new you. The Word of God tells us that in Christ we are new creatures. In order to walk in this newness, you have to have a renewed mind.

Roman 12:2, "Do not conform to the patterns of this world, but be transformed by the renewing of your mind. Then you will be able to test and approve what God's will is – his good, pleasing and perfect will."

We must live by the Spirit and not the flesh.

Galatians 5:16–26,

> "So I say, live by the Spirit, and you will not gratify the desires of the sinful nature. For the sinful nature desires what is contrary to the Spirit, and the Spirit what is contrary to the sinful nature. They are in conflict with each other, so that you do not do what you want. But if you are led by the Spirit, you are not under law. The acts of the sinful nature are obvious: sexual immorality, impurity and debauchery; idolatry and witchcraft; hatred, discord, jealousy, fits of rage, selfish ambition,

dissensions, factions and envy; drunkenness, orgies, and the like. I warn you, as I did before, that those who live like this will not inherit the kingdom of God. But the fruit of the Spirit is love, joy, peace, patience, kindness, goodness, faithfulness, gentleness and self-control. Against such things there is no law. Those who belong to Christ Jesus have crucified the sinful nature with its passions and desires. Since we live by the Spirit, let us keep in step with the Spirit. Let us not become conceited, provoking and envying each other."

Paul sets up two ways of living in Galatians 5:16–26:
- Walking in the Spirit
- Gratifying the desires of the flesh (sinful nature)

The acts associated with each are clear – works of the flesh, or sinful nature, in verses 19–21; and fruit of the Spirit in verses 22 and 23.

Paul knows that it is possible for Christians to live out of the sinful nature. Otherwise why would he urge them, "walk by the Spirit, and you will not gratify the desires of the sinful nature"? If it happened automatically he would not need to say this or warn them of the consequences of living that way.

However, Paul says that Christians should not live that way and do not have to. They have crucified the sinful nature by being united to Christ. This means that:

- The power of sin is broken in the cross (verse 24).
- The Spirit makes that victory a reality in our lives by transforming us step by step to become more like Jesus

The fruit of the Spirit (verses 22 and 23) is simply the character of Jesus formed in us by the Spirit.

Paul calls us to actively submit to the Spirit's transforming power as the means to overcome the power of sinful, unloving habits. The Spirit may work in us through various channels.

For Paul, a person who trusts in the gospel and is filled with the Spirit will live in a righteous way. So Paul now calls his converts to live lives compatible with their membership in God's family.

Faith naturally expresses itself in acts of love (Galatians 5:6), so Paul calls them to serve each other through love (v 13). By doing this they will fulfill the Law, which can be summed up by the love command.

Paul is saying that the real doers of the Law are actually people (including Gentiles) united to Christ, living by the Spirit, loving each other. So living by the Spirit empowers a lifestyle consistent with the ethical teaching of Jewish Law. This is why you need to be filled with the Holy Spirit. You cannot do it alone, you need the spirit of God to empower you and grow the fruits of the spirit within you, so you will not be led by the flesh.

Invitation to Heaven

I want to take this moment as your heart is in the right posture to receive, to invite you to Christ.

The only way to heaven is through Jesus Christ.

What must you do to be saved?

We must believe that Jesus died for our sins, and that He rose from the grave; and we must ask Jesus to forgive us for our sins, and accept Jesus as our Savior and our Lord.

Scriptures for Salvation

Romans 3:23, " For all have sinned and come short of the glory of God."

Romans 6:23, "For the wages of sin is death; but the gift of God is eternal life through Jesus Christ our Lord."

John 3:16, " For God so loved the world that he gave his only begotten son that whoever believes in him shall not perish but have eternal life."

John 14:6, "Jesus said, "I am the way, the truth, and the life: no man comes to the Father, but by me.""

Salvation Prayer Accepting Jesus Christ As My Saviour

Dear Heavenly Father, I believe that Jesus died for me. I believe that Jesus paid for my sins on the cross. I believe that Jesus rose from the dead. I ask you to forgive me of my sins. I ask you to wash me clean of all sin. I put my faith and trust in Jesus as my only hope for living eternally with you in heaven. I ask Jesus to be my Savior and my Lord. I want to live my life for Christ. I understand that my salvation is not based on my works but on the sacrifice of Jesus on the cross. Thank you for saving me! Amen!

Now Decree and Declare...I Know Who I Am In Christ!

- I am loved **(1 John 3:3)**
- I am a child of God **(John 1:12)**
- I am accepted **(Ephesians 1:6)**
- I am a friend of Jesus **(John 15:14)**
- I am called of God **(2 Timothy 1:9)**
- I am joint heirs with Jesus, sharing in his inheritance with Him **(Romans 8:17)**
- I am united with God and one with His Spirit **(1 Corinthians 6:17)**
- I am complete in Him **(Colossians 2:10)**
- I am strong in the Lord **(Ephesians 6:10)**
- I am a temple of God, His Spirit and His life

57

lives in me **(1 Corinthians 6:19)**
- I am a member of the Body of Christ **(1 Corinthians 12:27)**
- I am redeemed and forgiven **(Colossians 1:14)**
- I am redeemed from the curse of the law **(Galatians 3:13)**
- I am complete in Jesus Christ **(Colossians 2:10)**
- I am free from condemnation **(Romans 8:1)**
- I am a new creation because I am in Christ **(2 Corinthians 5:17)**
- I am chosen of God, holy and dearly loved **(Colossians 3:12)**
- I am healed by the stripes of Jesus **(1 Peter 2:24)**
- I am a son of God **(Galatians 4:7)**
- I am blessed **(Deuteronomy 28:2)**
- I am reconciled to God **(2 Corinthians 5:18)**
- I am a true worshiper who worships the Father in spirit and in truth **(John 4:8)**
- I am established, anointed and sealed by God **(2 Corinthians 1:21)**
- I am free from the spirit of fear because God has not given me a spirit of fear but of power, love and a sound mind **(2 Timothy 1:7)**

God wants us to be able to walk in His love, peace and joy. He wants us to be emotionally stable and for every negative thought to be removed from our minds. God is healing your mind and breaking all the old habits right now. He is giving you the strength and grace that you need to remove yourself from negative and toxic people and places. He is cutting every demonic soul tie.

In Jesus name, surround us Lord with people, places and opportunities that are conductive to our growth.

God is doing a new thing in you. It is time to leave the old ways behind you and try something new. Jesus has not left you all alone. It is vital that we learn to surrender our emotions to the Lord and not ignore them, but confront them. Sometimes Satan's goal is not to control our actions, but to make us inactive by making us believe that we don't have the self-belief to act for the Lord to make a difference and to move by faith. This is why I also included personal self-development and self-worth tactics. I believe God wants us to be balanced in every area of our lives.

Matthew 7:7-8 (NIV) encourages us to continue

seeking God. We must be consistent in our pressing towards the higher mark and remember that the Lord will reward us openly for what we do privately. Often we wait until the storms of life come before we start to pursue the face of God. But I pray throughout this 21-day transformational journey you will build a lifestyle of prayer and pursue the presence of God. I've learned throughout my own experiences that when we intentionally seek God and have a heart of thanksgiving towards Him, you build up walls of protection and put in place prevention mechanisms to block the enemy from entering your camp.

Matthew 7:7-8, *"Ask and it will be given to you; seek and you will find; knock and the door will be opened to you. For everyone who asks receives; the one who seeks finds; and the one who knocks, the door will be opened."*

I purposefully selected seven key scriptures for you to focus on everyday this week. I want to encourage you to read these scriptures over and over again for the next three weeks (21 days). Seven is the number of completion. I believe as you continually repeat this cycle over the next seven days for the next three weeks God is going to complete the good work He has started within you.

This 21 day transformational devotional has not been designed for you rush to through it. Take your time and meditate on each scripture and complete each exercise daily. Repetition allows the information to become your reality. I guarantee if you are consistent and persistent, these affirmations will change the way you think and speak, and will truly transform your life. Think of these devotionals as your daily prescription. Use them as often as you need to, to regain your peace and sustain your joy. Here are a few additional ways you can use these daily affirmations/scriptures effectively daily.

- Read one every day this week.

- Pick one and study it. Write down observations and applications.

- Memorize one of the scriptures.

- Share the scriptures to encourage yourself and others.

- Write it out and make it into a bookmark or affirmation cards.

- Pray the scriptures out loud.

- Believe you receive it and begin to thank God in advance by faith.

Learn to be thankful to God in all things, have a heart of thanksgiving.

Throughout this 21-day journey of transformation you will have time to reflect and journal the things you are thankful for. I firmly believe in the power of renewing your mind. You can start by entering into the presence of God. The Word of God says in Psalm 100:4, *"Enter His gates with thanksgiving and His courts with praise; give thanks to Him and bless His name."*

It's important that you enter each day with thanksgiving and praise to God. Before you ask Him for anything, learn how to be thankful for what you already have. Thanksgiving is expressing gratitude to God for everything He has given you. As believers our desire should be to develop a lifestyle of thanksgiving and attitude of gratitude for all the things He has done, whether those things are material, spiritual or physical. Our relationship with God should transform us into joyful, positive and grateful people.

In Luke 17 we see nine lepers that sadly represent most people's mindset or even our own at times. If we are not intentional about being thankful, we can become very ungrateful people because we are much better at murmuring and complaining than we are at truly being grateful.

The Word of God tells us that there were ten lepers who stood at a distance and cried out to Jesus as He was travelling along the border of Samaria and Galilee. They cried out, "Master have pity on us." Jesus heard the lepers and said to them promptly, "Go show yourselves to the priest." Luke 17:14-16 says, "And as the lepers went they were cleansed. "Out of the ten, one of them, when he saw he was healed, came back praising God in a loud voice. He threw himself at Jesus' feet and thanked him. In verses 17-18 Jesus says to the one leaper who returned, "Were not all ten cleansed? Where are the other nine? Was no one found to return and give praise to God except this foreigner?"

Jesus' response to the ungratefulness of the nine lepers gives us an indicator of our father's heart. Jesus was disappointed that only one came back to express his gratitude. So many times when people receive what they want, they never come back to say thank you and take what they received for granted.

Psalm 103:2, *"Bless the LORD, O my soul, and do not forget all His kind deeds."*

Be intentional to remember the blessings of God and remain thankful. Avoid complaining because it can be your greatest barrier to gratitude. Complaining will steal your peace.

Number 11:1, *"Soon the people began to complain about their hardship in the hearing of the LORD, and* when He heard them, His anger was kindled, and fire from the LORD blazed among them and consumed the outskirts of the camp."

It is so vital that we understand that complaining is like the plague, because God hates it and it ruins our spiritual development.

Psalms 77:3, "I remembered God, and was troubled: I complained, and my spirit was overwhelmed. Selah."

I pray this book is a tool to help you create a consistent pattern to quit complaining and start praising. Be intentional about thinking on the things that are good.

"Do everything without complaining or arguing, so that you may be blameless and pure, children of God without fault in a crooked and perverse generation, in which you shine as lights in the world."
– Philippians 2:14-15

Today I declare I am making the choice to rejoice!

Paul the apostle's words from prison were, "REJOICE IN THE LORD AND AGAIN I SAY REJOICE." You have to make the choice to rejoice and be glad despite your circumstances. Paul decided to praise

God regardless of his circumstances and it transformed his perspective. I want to challenge you today to give thanks daily. This book is designed to give you the blue print to transforming your life by transforming your mind. Gratitude is apart of that blueprint.

Here are a few more of my favorite scriptures to meditate on and declare when giving thanks to the Lord.

Ephesian 5:20, *"Always giving thanks to God the Father for everything, in the name of our LORD Jesus Christ."*

1 Chronicles 16:34 (NIV), *"Give thanks to the Lord, for he is good; his love endures forever."*

1 Thessalonians 5:18 (NIV), *"Give thanks in all circumstances; for this is God's will for you in Christ Jesus."*

Philippians 4:6 (NIV), *"Do not be anxious about anything, but in every situation, by prayer and petition, with thanksgiving, present your requests to God."*

All things are possible to those who believe. You have to activate your faith by visualizing yourself already having it, walking in it and living it.

What are you expecting?

_____
_____
_____
_____
_____
_____
_____
_____
_____

Write the vision and make it plain. Create a vision board.

Make a list of all the things you are thankful for.

_____
_____
_____
_____
_____
_____

Now that you have done this, you are ready to walk through the 21-days of renewing your mind.

7 Days of Renewing Your Mind

Week 1

Day 1

Ask the Lord to guard and direct your mind.

Scripture:

Romans 12:2 (NKJV), " And do not be conformed to this world, but be transformed by the renewing of your mind, that you may prove what is that good and acceptable and perfect will of God."

Prophetic Prayer

Thank you Lord for protecting and guarding my mind. I thank you that my mind is being transformed daily as I renew it in your Word. Lord, I thank you for my new mind in Christ. I put on the whole armor of God. I place the helmet of salvation on my head to block the enemy from my mind. I declare that my mind will be filled with wisdom, knowledge and understanding and I will meditate on things that are good. I soak my mind in the blood of Jesus Christ now and I cover my thoughts, my dreams, and my visions under Your Blood. Lord, thank you for upgrading my thinking. Remove every limitation and every barrier. I speak to every crooked place in my mind and I declare by the power of the Holy Ghost that it is being made straight now in Jesus Name. My mind is in total alignment with your Word, will, plans and purpose for my life, Amen.

Lord, Today I Am Thankful For...

_____

_____

_____

_____

_____

_____

_____

_____

_____

_____

_____

Day 2

Be intentional about knowing the voice of God. Ask the Lord to amplify His voice in your mind.

Scripture:

John 10:27 (NKJV), "My sheep hear My voice, and I know them, and they follow Me."

John 10:5 (NKJV), "Yet they will by no means follow a stranger, but will flee from him, for they do not know the voice of strangers."

Prophetic Prayer

Lord I thank you for opening my ears to hear your voice and to not be led away by the voice of a stranger. I declare my ears will be inclined to your voice Lord. I silence the voice of the enemy that has come to kill, steal and destroy. Lord I surrender all. Lead me and guide me. Be my spiritual navigation system in the spiritual realm now. I know you are the Good Shepherd that laid down your life for me. I thank you for watching over me and protecting me from wolves in sheep's clothing and giving me the discernment to recognize the lies of the enemy. I come out of agreement with every demonic contract made knowingly or unknowingly and I cancel it now in Jesus name. I thank you for setting me free Lord and giving me a mind like Christ, renewed by your

Spirit through your Word. I thank you Lord for amplifying your voice in my mind today. I trust and obey you, let your will be done. Amen.

Lord, Today I Am Thankful For...

_____

_____

_____

_____

_____

_____

_____

_____

_____

_____

_____

_____

Day 3

Draw close to the Lord and as you submit yourself to Him, ask Him to give you the strength and power you need, by His Holy Spirit, to resist the devil so he can flee.

Scripture:

James 4:7-8 (NKJV), "Therefore, submit to God. Resist the devil and he will flee from you. Draw near to God and He will draw near to you. Cleanse your hands, you sinners; and purify your heart you double-minded."

Prophetic Prayer

Lord I humbly submit myself to you. I submit my mind, body and soul to you Lord. I am committed to your agenda. I am totally in agreement with your will. Lord I surrender my will to you today. Teach me your ways. Send your Helper to guide and direct me. I thank you that I am drawing closer and closer to you every day, and that I am abiding in your Word and you are abiding in me. I thank you for cleansing my mind. I thank you for healing me in my spirit. I thank you for healing me in my mind. I thank you for healing me in my body. I thank you for healing me in my soul. I thank you for cleansing me and purifying me, and for stabilizing my mind from all double-mindedness that I might be steadfast, unmovable and unshakable, rooted and grounded in your Word and love. I declare that as I submit to you Lord, the devil will flee from every area of my life and he will find no entry point to return. I empty myself of everything that is not of you and invite you to fill me up with your Spirit until I overflow with the fullness of the Spirit of God. According to your Word in Isaiah 11, let your Spirit rest on me and dwell through me in Jesus name, Amen.

Lord, Today I Am Thankful For...

_____

_____

_____

_____

_____

_____

_____

_____

_____

_____

_____

Day 4

There is power of life and death in your tongue. Ask the Lord to give you discernment to recognize the lies of the enemy, so that you can replace it with truth from the Word of God.

Scripture:

Proverbs 18:21 (NKJV), " Death and life are in the power of the tongue, And those who love it will eat its fruit."

Prophetic Prayer

Lord I thank you for giving me the power of life and death in my tongue. Lord I thank you for giving me wisdom to speak life and to speak what I want to manifest in my life, family, business and ministry. Lord I thank you for teaching me to speak good things and to think of things that are of good report. I thank you for stretching my faith as I read and speak all of these prophetic affirmations, prayers and scriptures. I believe that I will see the fruit of them in every area of my life. I declare that this will help me to go deeper in you Lord and be the best version of myself and I will maximize my full potential and fulfill my God given purpose. I declare I will be purpose driven, move boldly and fearless, and be confident in You. I have put on the mind of Christ and I am intentional about speaking good in my life regardless of what I am up against. I have faith to overcome and be victorious because I am not trusting in myself, but I put all my trust in You, Lord. Yes, I declare I have godly confidence, and I will worship you daily in Spirit and in truth. Amen

Lord, Today I Am Thankful For...

Day 5

Filter your mind daily by refocusing your thoughts ad intentionally training your mind to think on the things of God and not be consumed by the things of the world.

Scripture:

Colossians 3:1-2 (NKJV), " If then you were raised with Christ, seek those things which are above, where Christ is, sitting at the right hand of God. Set your mind on things above, not on things on the earth."

Romans 8:5-7 (NKJV), " For those who live according to the flesh set their minds on the things of the flesh, but those who live according to the Spirit, the things of the Spirit. For to be [a] carnally minded is death, but to be spiritually minded is life and peace."

Prophetic Prayer

Lord I thank you for filtering my mind, and for washing out every seed planted by the enemy of pain, rejection, disappointment, doubt, fear, anxiety, insecurity, torment, guilt, shame, hopelessness and everything that is not like you. Lord, I thank you for reconstructing my thoughts to be in alignment with your Word, so I will think on the things above and not on earth. I thank you Lord for filling me with peace, love, joy, faith, hope and a sound mind in Jesus name. I thank you Lord that I will set my mind on the things of the Spirit that springs forth life and not the flesh. I pray that every day you will increase the fruits of the Spirit within me and that I will be fruitful in every area of my life. I will walk by faith and not by sight and I will be a living testimony of your love, grace and mercy. In Jesus name, Amen.

Lord, Today I Am Thankful For...

_____

_____

_____

_____

_____

_____

_____

_____

_____

_____

_____

Day 6

Rest in the truth that you are accepted in Jesus Christ. When your thoughts of faith are in Jesus, you are at peace with God and you are a son of God, free from accusation.

Scripture:

2 Peter 1:5 (NKJV), " But also for this very reason, giving all diligence, add to your faith virtue, and to virtue knowledge."

Romans 8: 1 (NKJV), " There is therefore now no condemnation to those who are in Christ Jesus, who[a\ do not walk according to the flesh, but according to the Spirit."

Prophetic Prayer

I thank you Lord for giving me freedom in you. I thank you that no weapon formed against me will prosper and every negative tongue that has risen up against me, I condemn now in Jesus name. I declare total wholeness, divine health, wealth, favor, blessings, protection, recognition, provision and wisdom in every area of my life. I declare as I walk according to the Spirit and not the flesh, that my feet will be ordered by the Lord and I will enjoy the goodness of the Lord in the land of the living. Lord as you have turned my darkness into marvelous light, empower me to help others see the light in me and accept you and your truth. I declare the good work you have started in my life will come to completion and I am no longer a prisoner to my past but have been set free from sin, bondage, sickness, and fear. I am loosed from Satan, and he is no longer my master. I cut all ties, demolish all strongholds, break all chains and renounce all contracts in the mighty name of Jesus. I declare that I will remain free and will not go back and be entangled again because Jesus has set me free and whom the Son sets free is free indeed. I thank you that there is no condemnation to those who are in Christ Jesus. Amen.

Lord, Today I Am Thankful For...

_____

_____

_____

_____

_____

_____

_____

_____

_____

_____

Day 7

Declare your **I Am Affirmations**.

I Am Affirmations to Transform Your Life

- I am setting my mind on the things above, and not beneath.
- I am saved.
- I am putting on the mind of Christ.
- I am free from condemnation.
- I am delivered from the power of darkness and translated into God's Kingdom.
- I am the temple of the Holy Ghost.
- I am born of God and the evil one does not touch me.
- I am an ambassador of Christ.
- I am fearless.
- I am faithful.
- I am blessed.
- I am beautiful.
- I am courageous.
- I am unstoppable.
- I am victorious
- I am called of God.
- I am reconciled to God.
- I am chosen.
- I am redeemed.
- I am set free.
- I am the head and not the tail.
- I am sealed with the Holy Spirit of promise.

- I am the salt of the earth.
- I am a partner of His divine nature.
- I am loved.
- I am accepted.
- I am gifted.
- I am anointed.
- I am healed.
- I am restored.
- I am his faithful follower.
- I am healed by the stripes of Jesus.
- I am changed into the image of Christ.
- I am dead to sin and alive to God.
- I am qualified to share in his inheritance.
- I am successful.
- I am whole.
  I am confident.
- I am forgiven.
- I am grateful.
- I am strong.
- I am generous.
- I am favoured.
- I am powerful.
- I am more than a conqueror.
- I am ready for change.
- I am attracting divine connections.
- I am attracting divine connections.
- I am attracting more abundance, prosperity and wealth.
- I am prosperous.

- I am open to receive love.
- I am positioned to continue winning.
- I am open to receive abundance without limits.
- I am firmly rooted, built up, established in my faith and overflowing with gratitude.
- I am God's masterpiece.
- I am built upon the foundations of the apostles and prophets, Jesus Christ Himself being the chief cornerstone.

Whatever your mind can conceive you will receive. Your thoughts are what bring you up or keep you down. It's the level that you think at that can limit the move of God in your life. Think of it like this, your mind can either be a womb springing forth life or a tomb carrying death, what are you expecting? Do you have the courage to think beyond where you are? Your perception has everything to do with your progression. The power of renewing your mind is strategically giving you the ammunition you need to reload your weapon on the enemy trying to take over the territory in your mind.

Today you need to believe you will receive it by faith without doubting. Using this technique for the next 21-days, will help you to actively put your faith into action.

Prophetic Prayer

Lord I pray that you will forgive me and have mercy on me for anything that I have done that has not been in your will. I pray that you will reset, renew and regulate my mind according to your will. Fill my mind with your wisdom, knowledge and understanding. Help me to recognize the whispers of the enemy and renounce and replace every lie with the truth in your Word. Keep my mind focused on you Lord. Give me the faith, endurance, and the perseverance I need to manifest your glory on earth. Remove every scale right now. In Jesus name, open the eyes of my understanding. Lord, let there be light. Let the light of your truth be my guide. Thank you for empowering me with your Spirit to comfort me, help me and direct me through this narrow path. Continue to order my footsteps Lord and put the whole armor of God on me, as I know this fight is not against flesh and blood, but principalities and powers in high places. Cover me and my family with your precious blood. I decree that I have the mind of Christ, and that I will think on the things above and not beneath. I will be about my father's business. You have not given me a spirit of fear, but power, love and a sound mind. I thank you Lord that your love casts out all fear. I thank you Lord for giving me a new mindset, a new spirit, and a new heart. I thank you for your transformational power, and for giving me a supernatural brain transplant, removing my old mind and giving me the mind of Christ. Let your will be done on earth, as it is in heaven. In Jesus name, Amen.

Prophetic Decree

In the Name of Jesus I release the blessings of the Lord over you today. According to His Word In Deuteronomy as you are obedient to Him, all these blessings will overtake you and your family. Please continue to confess theses scriptures daily as you trust and obey God, and watch how quickly they will manifest in your life. Obedience equals blessings and disobedience will result in curses according to Deuteronomy 28:1-14.

Lord, Today I Am Thankful For...

_____
_____
_____
_____
_____
_____
_____
_____
_____
_____
_____

Week 2

Repeat Days 1-7. Additional pages are available in the back of the book to jot down the things you are grateful for.

Week 3

Repeat Days 1-7. Additional pages are available in the back of the book to jot down the things you are grateful for.

Remember that God sees all and knows all. God has you covered, so no weapon formed against you shall prosper. Don't believe the lies of the enemy, and be careful who you lend your ear to. Stop listening to what people say, and pay attention to what they do. Surround yourself with what you want to become, not who you currently are

.

1 Corinthians 15:33, *"Don't be fooled by those who say such things, for bad company corrupts good character."*

Proverbs 13:20, *"Walk with the wise and become wise; associate with fools and get into trouble."*

My Circle Evaluation

Does my current circle add any value to my life, business or ministry?

_____
_____
_____
_____
_____
_____

Is there anyone in my circle I need to disconnect from or spend less time communicating with?

_____
_____
_____
_____
_____
_____

What qualities does my current circle have?

_____
_____
_____
_____
_____
_____

Is there anyone in my current circle that can mentor me?

_____

_____

_____

_____

_____

_____

Is there anyone in my current circle that is more educated, successful or influential than me?

_____

_____

_____

_____

_____

What action steps can I make today to ensure I have balance in my circle?

_____

_____

_____

_____

_____

What 3 goals can I set today to invest in my circle growing healthy?

_____

_____

_____

_____

_____

_____

It is important that you have a balanced circle in order to grow healthy and not become stagnant or drained. I had to go through the process myself to cut off some old friends, family and people that were adding no value to my life, but opening the door to negativity and doubt. You have to be willing to close the door to the dream killers in your life, so the door can be opened to your divine connections, those sent by God to push you into your destiny.

I had to be intentional about my growth and invest in courses, training programs and coaches in different areas of my life to ensure I was being developed and growing daily to reach my full potential. I had to submit to leadership and be held accountable. I believe your circle should be balanced and you should defiantly set boundaries and know that your time is valuable. Once again this comes with having the right mindset and knowing your worth. If you do this, you won't settle for less. You need those above you who inspire you to be greater, you need those on your level so that you can encourage each other and you need those that are under you, that you can inspire and encourage to be greater. Are you ready to open the door to people who will inspire, encourage and stretch you to become greater? You need to be around people that have greater wisdom, experience, education, and influence than you. If you are the smartest person in your circle, I'm sorry to tell you that you are in the wrong circle.

It is time to start building new connections with like-minded people.

You can start by joining our Facebook community **@thepowerofrenewingyourmind**

Recommended Books

The Holy Bible

Turning Point- Venesia Williams

Pigs In the Parlor- Frank and Ida Mae Hammond

The 40-day Soul Fast- Dr. Cindy Trimm

Faithing It- Cora Jakes Coleman

The Greatest You- Trent Shelton

Believe Bigger- Marshawn Evans Daniels

Next Level Beautiful- Tawanda La'Shun Usher

Burn for Jesus- Carla R. Cannon

Let God Fight Your Battles- Joyce Meyers

Commanding Your Morning- Dr. Cindy Trimm

Soar- Bishop T.D. Jakes

Secrets of A Prayer Warrior- Derek Prince

Just Enough Light for the Step I'm On- Stormie Omartian

Maximizing Your Full Potential- Dr. Myles Munroe

Prayer That Brings Change- Kimberly Daniels

The God Chaser- Tommy Tenny

Battlefield of the Mind- Joyce Meyers

The Journey- Bryan Meadows

The Cave- Bryan Meadows

Be confident in calling your daddy by His names. Each redemptive name reveals how God can meet every need of His people with His power.

Names Relating to God's Fatherhood

My Father, and your Father (John 20:17)
Abba, Father/ Daddy God (Galatians 4:6; Romans 8:15)
God our Father (1 Corinthians 1:3)
The Father of glory (Ephesians 1:17)
God is light and He is love (1 John 1:5, 4:8)
The God and Father of our Lord Jesus Christ (1 Peter 1:3)
The father of lights (James 1:17)
The Father of spirits (Hebrews 12:9)
God the Father (Galatians 1:3)
The Father of mercies, The God of all comfort
(2 Corinthians 1:3)
One God, the Father, of whom are all things
(1 Corinthians 8:6)
Father of all, who is above all, and through all, and in you all (Ephesians 4:6)

There is power in His NAME at His NAME every knee shall bow and every tongue confess that He is LORD.

JESUS, JESUS, JESUS, JESUS... Call out His Name, Jesus, there is power in His NAME!

Other Titles and Names of God

YHWH (LORD) – The self-existent One revealing Himself to His people in redemptive purpose.

YHWH Shammah- The Lord is there, ever present. (Ezekiel 48:35)

YHWH Tsuri v'goali- The Lord My Rock and Redeemer (Psalm 19:14)

YHWH Sal'i- The Lord My Rock (Psalm 18:2)

YHWH Gibbor- The Lord is Mighty (Deuteronomy 10:17)

YHWH Tsidkenu- The Lord our Righteousness (Jeremiah 23:6)

YHWH Raah / Roi – The Lord my Shepherd (Psalm 23:1)

YHWH Elohim- The Lord God Redeemer Creator (Genesis 2:4)

YHWH Elohim Tseva'ot- The Lord of Hosts (Psalm 84:8, Jeremiah 15:16)

YHWH Elohai- The Lord My God (Psalm 13:3)

YHWH Osenu- The Lord Our Maker (Psalm 95:6)

YHWH Jireh- The Lord Who Sees and Provides (Genesis 22:14)

YHWH Elyon- The Lord Most High (Psalm 7:17)

YHWH Rapha- The Lord Who Heals (Exodus 15:26)

YHWH Nissi- The Lord my Banner (Exodus 17:15

YHWH Kanna- The Lord who is Jealous (Exodus 20:5)

YHWH M'kaddesh- The Lord who sanctifies (Leviticus 20:8)

YHWH Shalom- The Lord our Peace (Judges 6:24)

YHWH Shaphat- The Lord is Judge

EL = To be strong, powerful, or mighty.
Elohim- The Creator God (Genesis 1:1)
El Echad- The One God (Malachi 1:1)
El Hanne'eman- The Faithful God (Deuteronomy 7:9)

El Emet- The God of Truth (Psalm 31:5)

El-Beth-El- The God of the House of God (Genesis 31:13)

El Tsaddik- The Righteous God (Isaiah 45:21)

El Shaddai- The All Sufficient, Many Breasted (Genesis 17:1)

Elohim T'Sabaoth- Master, Ruler of All (Amos 4:13, Romans 9:29)

El Hannora- The Awesome God (Nehemiah 9:32)

El-Elohe-Isreal- God The God of Israel (Genesis 33:20)

Elohim-Elyon- God The Most High God (Psalm 91:1-2)

El Elyon- The Most High God (Genesis 14:20, Psalm 9:2)

El Roi- The God who Sees Me (Genesis 16:13-14)

El Olam- The Everlasting God (Genesis 21:33)

El Gibbor- The Mighty God (Isaiah 9:6)

El De'ot- The God of Knowledge (1 Samuel 2:3)

El Haggadol- The Great God (Deuteronomy 10:17)

El –Kanna- The Jealous God (Exodus 20:5, Deuteronomy 4:24)

El Yeshuatenu- The God of Our Salvation (Psalm 68:19)

El Yeshuati- The God of My Salvation (Isaiah 12:2)

El Rachum- The God of Compassion and Mercy (Deuteronomy 4:31)

El Channum- The Gracious God (Jonah 4:2)

El Chaiyai- The God of My Life (Psalm 42:8)

El Haggadol- The Great God (Deuteronomy 10:17)

El Hakkavod- The Holy God (Isaiah 5:16)

El Hashamayim- The God of the Heavens (Psalm 136:26)

Immanu-el- God is with us (Isaiah 7:14)

Connect With Venesia

@yourempowermentcoachvenesia
@thepoweroflloveministry

@beingvenesiawilliams

@thepoweroflove_min

@thepoweroflove_min

@thepoweroflove_min

I would love to work with you and give you the strategies you need to maximize your full potential.

Contact me personally to receive your one on one empowerment online session at www.venesiawilliams.com

For ministry bookings/speaking engagements/workshops/seminars/conferences- please contact me on my website, www.thepoweroflloveministry.com

Lord, Today I Am Thankful For...

_____

_____

_____

_____

_____

_____

_____

_____

_____

_____

_____

_____

_____

Lord, Today I Am Thankful For...

_____

_____

_____

_____

_____

_____

_____

_____

_____

_____

_____

_____

_____

Lord, Today I Am Thankful For...

_____

_____

_____

_____

_____

_____

_____

_____

_____

_____

_____

_____

Lord, Today I Am Thankful For...

_____

_____

_____

_____

_____

_____

_____

_____

_____

_____

_____

_____

Lord, Today I Am Thankful For...

_____

_____

_____

_____

_____

_____

_____

_____

_____

_____

_____

_____

Lord, Today I Am Thankful For...

_____

_____

_____

_____

_____

_____

_____

_____

_____

_____

_____

_____

Lord, Today I Am Thankful For...

_____
_____
_____
_____
_____
_____
_____
_____
_____
_____
_____
_____

Lord, Today I Am Thankful For...

_____
_____
_____
_____
_____
_____
_____
_____
_____
_____
_____
_____

Lord, Today I Am Thankful For...

_____

_____

_____

_____

_____

_____

_____

_____

_____

_____

_____

_____

Lord, Today I Am Thankful For...

_____

_____

_____

_____

_____

_____

_____

_____

_____

_____

_____

_____

Lord, Today I Am Thankful For...

_____

_____

_____

_____

_____

_____

_____

_____

_____

_____

_____

_____

_____

Lord, Today I Am Thankful For...

_____

_____

_____

_____

_____

_____

_____

_____

_____

_____

_____

_____

Lord, Today I Am Thankful For...

_____

_____

_____

_____

_____

_____

_____

_____

_____

_____

_____

Lord, Today I Am Thankful For...

_____

_____

_____

_____

_____

_____

_____

_____

_____

_____

_____

48406980R00060

Printed in Poland
by Amazon Fulfillment
Poland Sp. z o.o., Wrocław